Gas Station

Etiquette

I0181970

Iris Berry

Punk ★ Hostage ★ Press

Gas Station Etiquette

Cover Layout
Iris Berry
Johnny Indovina

Illustrations
Scott Aicher

Special Thank Yous to:
Joe Donnelly, Sean Wheeler,
Amanda "Mandy" Toland,
Judy Horsefield, Debbie Dexter Shaffer
Johnny Indovina, and Lola.

Punk Hostage Press
Hollywood, California
punkhostagepress.com

For

Luis Rodriguez and A. Razor

Contents

Leave room for the magic…

Most of the gas stations in Los Angeles manage to take on the flavor of their locations. And along with the people that work in them, you might say they take on the souls of their neighborhoods.

Gas Station Etiquette

Once I'm inside, I can never tell the difference between a Right Aid and a CVS, or a Starbucks and a Coffee Bean, they're all the same. But I can't say that about the gas stations here in Los Angeles. They all have their own personalities. And the thing about L.A. is it's so spread out that sometimes a gas station can be the only place a person can have any social interactions all day, at all.

I have my favorites. There's about 10 of them. And I will drive out of my way just to go to a specific one.

The gas station down the street from me bakes all their own pastries onsite. People come from miles around 8pm nightly because they know that's when the precious baked goods come fresh and hot out of the oven.

And the ones that have a drive through car wash are always a plus! It's like a ride at a carnival, and where I get some of my best thinking done. Some of them have the kind of stores in their AM/PM's where you can get anything from great sunglasses to CBD edibles, nicotine patches and even clothing. Not that I would buy my clothes at an AM/PM. But some of that stuff is actually pretty cute.

There's a gas station on Sepulveda Blvd. that sits somewhere between the San Fernando Valley and Westwood Village right in the shadow of the Getty Museum and the 405 Freeway. It has a huge section of gluten-free really delicious cookies and candies, only in L.A would there be a need for a section like this. I like to call this *Gas Station Gourmet*.

There's another gas station on Ventura Blvd. in Woodland Hills where you can get your car detailed with a waiting area that has about 10 massage chairs and a wall size big screen TV, with a little boutique connected to it that sells designer bathing suits and evening gowns. They stay in business, so, someone's buying that stuff.

Most of the gas stations in Los Angeles manage to take on the flavor of their locations. And along with the people that work in them, you might say they take on the souls of their neighbourhoods.

In July of 2018 I took the Amtrak to San Luis Obispo to visit my brother Marty. It was a weekend getaway. A lovely place to visit and live. On the train ride back home, after boarding the train at 6am, we make a stop in Goleta. I'm sitting next to this very interesting European woman in her mid sixties. I first notice her when she's dropped off at the station by her 20 something skater-punk boyfriend,

Hmm, what's going on here?

When the train stops in Goleta, she, and I both get off to have a smoke. We talk for a quick minute when the conductor announces,

"All aboard."

"After you," I say to her.

She gets on and just as I'm about to follow her onto the train, the sliding glass doors start to close. So, I put my hand in between the closing doors to stop them, like I would with an elevator door. Only my hand doesn't stop the doors. They close right on it. The European women starts freaking out. I'm just stunned. All my luggage is on that train, and I'm not.

As I watch the train chug off down the tracks, I can't believe my eyes. It's 6:45 in the morning and I'm now stuck in the Goleta train station 81 miles away from home. Calling it a train station is generous. Really, it's a lonely bus bench surrounded by a vast industrial area, and that's it. Oh, and two women with a literature rack filled with Jehovah's Witness pamphlets asking me if I've heard the good word of the Lord.

"Have you let the Lord in your heart today?"

"Yeah, yeah, sure, sure, no problem. But do you know when the next train is coming?"

Neither one of them have a clue about trains, just the Lord.

Did I mention my phone is about to die and I really have to go to the bathroom...

Lucky for me, I've got three great older brothers who will help me with just about anything. And the big questions are which brother do I call first before my phone dies? And where is the nearest bathroom? I call Marty, the brother who just dropped me off. Tell him what's happening, and *HELP!*

As I'm walking around aimlessly trying to find any place that might have a bathroom and an outlet to charge my phone, Marty is calling my two other brothers to make some kind of rescue plan for me.

With three percent of battery life left on my phone I just keep walking and walking through what seems to be a deserted industrial area.

Obviously, it's too early for people to be at work. The hope is to find some kind of civilization, like a Denny's or something.

Goleta is one of those places where the population gets lower every year. *No surprise here.* Right then, it was at a cool 30,000, compare that to the Los Angeles population of 4 million, and you can get an idea of what I was dealing with.

After walking about a mile, out of the comer of my eye I spot a Radisson Hotel in the distance, hoping it's not a mirage. It's odd, because the closer I get I notice the parking lot is completely empty.

Is this place even in business? Is this town even inhabited?

I enter the lobby of the Hotel and there's one extremely cold (almost robotic) person working the front desk of a huge lobby with big Screen TVs everywhere, blasting to no one. *But* all the free hot fresh coffee I can drink with a more than ample supply of vanilla creamer. About 20 empty hightop tables and each one has a place to charge my phone. And there's a bathroom the size of a small backyard, and it's nice! Just in the nick of time, (I might Add).

Have I died and gone to heaven? My bar

for Heaven is pretty low at this point.

When I get Marty back on the phone, he's got a rescue plan in place. He's on his way to come get me and drive me to the Santa Barbara train station, while my brother Don has already spoke with the Amtrak people and arranged to pick-up my luggage when the train hits the Canoga Park station. And my brother Paul will pick me up at my new arrival time. This is a great plan!

After Marty and I have a lovely lunch in Santa Barbara, he puts me on the train and I'm happily heading for home. Don will get my luggage from the 12-noon train and Paul will pick me up at 4:30 pm. I can relax now.

As the train is pulling into the Canoga Park station, I hear the conductor say,

"Next stop Canoga Park."

I get up with a sigh of relief and head for the exit. There's only one problem, I can't find an exit. I'm frantically running all over the train.

What the fuck!!!! First, I can't get back on the train and now I can't get off??!!

The train takes off with me still in it! At this point I grab the conductor by his lapels screaming,

"Let me off this fucking train!"

He isn't real happy or helpful. It's like some sort of *Twilight Zone* episode.

Now I'm just in tears. I call my brother Paul, sobbing. He's much calmer than I am and says not to worry, he'll pick me up at the next stop which is in Van Nuys at 5:20 pm.

Oh My God, will this train ride ever end?!

When we pull up to the Van Nuys station I'm camped out at the exit. The door opens and I'm off that train at warp speed. All manors and decorum are out the window.

Do not get in my way!

***

Paul eventually shows up but needs to make one stop.

.   *Ugh, I just want to go home…*

But beggars can't be choosers, right? So, while he's picking up paperwork from a client in some Highrise, I'm in the car waiting, driving around and around the block because there's nowhere to park 'South of the Boulevard' in Van Nuys. And I have to go to the bathroom, *again*, with nowhere to go, *again,* when I spot a gas station on the corner of Van Nuys Blvd. and Riverside Drive.

I go inside and I'm greeted by this beautiful middle eastern woman working the counter of the AM/PM. She's immaculately dressed from head to toe in her homeland attire with a lovely sparkling bhindi on her forehead. I'm praying they have a

working bathroom and it's available to the public.
I sheepishly ask her,

"Do you have a bathroom, and if so, can I
use it?"

"You got it *sister-girl*, straight back and on
you're right."

Her kindness is music to my ears. Making
me feel at home (finally) and safe...

For as long as I can remember people have
talked shit about how L.A. is such a rude an un-
friendly city. I'm gonna beg to differ. Maybe it's
just where you go and who you talk to. Maybe be-
cause Los Angeles is a melting pot of all different
kinds of people speaking different languages. May-
be we're all stuck in our cars too long, alone and
frustrated while the car in front of us is texting
when they should be making that left-hand turn
into a parking garage. And maybe on these lonely
endless roads where freedom seems to be at the
next exit, and probably at the next gas station, I
should be a little nicer, because these people work-
ing at these gas stations see it all and field it all
from the front lines of the emotional temperature
of a city that's extremely overcrowded and over-
priced. And this woman is being kinder to me than
any other stranger I've encountered outside of Los
Angeles on this whole insane day.

***

As I'm leaving the AM/PM a homeless man walks ahead of me and says,

"Allow me *madame*, let me get that for you."

As he puts his foot down to trigger the electric doors to open in front of me, the doors open.

And he extends his arms in a chivalrous manner to signify *after you*. I giggle and he smiles. And I think to myself,

Home is where the doors open.
There really is no place like home.
I love L.A.

In Search of the Perfect Emoji

in the time it takes
searching
for the right exact
emoji
for how I feel
about you
about me
about us
what's safe
and what isn't
all that time spent
collectively
I could have
learned another language
baked many cakes
done several good deeds
redecorated my house
we could've gone to the movies
many times
and had numerous conversations
well into the early morning hours…
but instead
here we are
divided by screens
and fear of being
vulnerable
where's the emoji for that…

Leave Room for the Magic

Some days
the easiest task
can feel so hard
traffic can feel unbearable
the phone doesn't ring
so, I shake it
like it's an Etch A Sketch
making sure it's not broken
my car is so dirty
I can't bear
to be in it
and the world feels
like there's no hope
at all.

And then the very next day
nothing's changed
my car is still dirty
if not dirtier
traffic is still awful and rude
if not ruder
the world still has all the same
problems as yesterday
but none of it bothers me
it's just another day
with just a little bit more magic…

L.A. River Lullaby

It's 2:06 am
I can hear the sounds
of a distant train
as the constant passing of cars
drive the 5 freeway
alongside the L.A. River
heading north
and heading south
going to places called home.
Home for me
is not a place

with walls
windows and doors
where framed photographs
are placed on mantles
over fireplaces
and lined hallways
or embedded
in refrigerator magnets.

Home lives in my heart
and in my breath
and in the unsaid exchange
of knowing glimpses
with loved ones
and kindred spirits
ignited by
the reciprocity
of trust
kindness
safety
love
and the generosity
of a spirit
that goes beyond
material items.
Beyond
coaxing words
and gestures
for planned outcomes

beyond any exchange
of anything
wanted
or needed.

Home is not
the room
for the life
but for the life
in the room.

Home lives
in the conversations
that our souls
are having
with each other
without words
where truths
are unspoken
with an unconditional love
that rings louder
and with more power
than mere words
could ever express
with an emanating
everlasting
unstoppable
force.

Home is anywhere
the heart thrives…

As the passing cars
on the 5 freeway
get quieter and quieter
until all I can hear
is the distant train
and the unspoken words.

For all the Perfect Moments...

nothing hurts
inside or out
I feel safe and good
I look around and
all I see is beauty
I feel at one
with the trees
and the flowers
the air is soft
and still
and quiet
I'm alone
but not lonely
I feel connected
to everything
good
and I'll take it...

sometimes
it's that one perfect moment
that can make up for
all the other painfully
not so perfect...

Tuesdays on Fairfax with Mom...

Every Tuesday
rain or shine
we'd go
to Canter's Delicatessen
and sit in one of those
big round booths
in the main

dining room
in the very back
so we could see
the whole restaurant
at a glance.

And she'd tell me stories
about my dad
and how he worked there
back in the 1950s
when it was called Cohen's
when he moved
the whole family
out to sunny California
from the East Coast
and stories
about my brothers
all before I was born.
And we'd laugh
till we cried.

And then
we'd go over
to Farmer's Market
on 3rd & Fairfax
and sit outside
drinking cappuccinos

every Tuesday
rain or shine...
and we didn't even care
if we got rained on
we were too busy
laughing till we cried.

How to Outrun the Slow Death of Your Mom

Stop sleeping
stay awake
stay distracted
or sleep too much
never get out of bed
stay in your pajamas
watch bad TV
watch good TV
watch old movies
watch anything
that has
nothing to do
with your life.

Do whatever
it takes
to not feel
chain smoke
do too much
for other people
people who didn't
ask for your help
and when they don't
appreciate you
get really mad at them

for not being psychic
about
how
you've helped them.
Don't pay attention
to serious conversations
that have
anything to do
with your
dying mom.

Take on
as many projects
as possible
paint the kitchen floor
clean out
your closet
but don't throw
anything away
especially
the useless stuff
like phone numbers
on napkins
from people
you don't
remember
meeting.

Make plans

but don't
keep them
don't return
phone calls
especially
if they want
to talk about
your dying mom
no one
really wants
to hear
about it
it's too close
to home
we all
have mothers
some dead
and some
still alive
we all die
and it makes
people
uncomfortable
they only ask
because they don't
want to seem
like they don't care
but they
will only

say things
that hurt
you more
they don't mean to
because most people
don't know
what you are
really going through.
Stop being serious
listen only
to people
who are drunk
and don't want
to talk about
your dying mom.

Get in fights
with people
you love
over little things
like the dishes
or the trash
don't talk to
family members
who bug you
or don't
celebrate you
the ones who
want to

tell you
how to
live your life,
because it's impossible
for them
to know
so, you won't listen
and it will only
bug them more
so just
avoid them
all together.

Change everything
about your life
move
get a new job
sign on dotted lines
but don't read
the fine print.
Look hours
for things
you know
you will
never find.
If you drink alcohol
drink more
but don't
drink and drive

one death
is enough
if you don't
drink alcohol
then eat
and eat badly
sugar
starch
salt
and eat a lot of it
and make sure
it's not good for you
candy for breakfast
dessert for dinner
eat anything
that can't outrun you
and doesn't taste
like cardboard.

Frequent See's Candy
so much
that you know each other
on a first name basis.
Live way beyond
your means
use all your credit cards
max them out
buy stuff
you don't need

and let your temper
get the best of you.
Cuss and say things
you normally wouldn't
let your lower self
run the show
cuss people out
in traffic
drive fast
and tell people off
tell your friends off
tell them
what you've really
been thinking
all these years
get it out
get it all out
because in the end
after all this blows over
this *is* the only time
most people
will give
you a pass…

About the Author

Iris Berry is a native Angeleno and one of the founding creative minds behind Punk Hostage Press. She is the author of several books and has appeared in numerous films, TV commercials, documentaries, and iconic rock videos. In the 1980s she was a singer for the punk band the Lame Flames. Later, Berry co-founded The Ringling Sisters, who recorded with legendary producer Lou Adler (A&M Records). Berry also sang and wrote songs and recorded with the Dickies, the Flesh Eaters and Pink Sabbath. She's received two certificates of merit from the city of Los Angeles for her contribution as a Los Angeles writer, and for her extensive charity work. In 2010 she served four years on the Board of Directors for Beyond Baroque Literary/Arts Center. In 2012 on Friday the 13th of January Iris, along with A. Razor launched PUNK HOSTAGE PRESS. Where she continues to champion and advocate for original voices.

About The Illustrator

Scott Aicher's love for art began at the early age of five when he won 3 blue ribbons after his mother entered his paintings in a local art show. Largely a self-taught artist, he has had many years of experience as a professional artist starting in humble print shops, then later advancing to illustration for entertainment, record and surf companies. Scott's work can be seen on various flyers and record covers for: Bad Religion, Pennywise, Firehose, Chemical People, Jeff Dahl, Rikk Agnew, TSOL, the Angry Samoans, Chicano Batman, Mike Watt, Toys That Kill, Rolling Blackouts, Love Canal, Blood on the Saddle, Left Insane and Nip Drivers to name a few. Along with illustrating two books by TSOL front man Jack Grisham, *Untamed* and *Code Blue* (Punk Hostage Press). And Iris Berry's *All That Shines Under the Hollywood Sign* and *The Trouble with Palm Trees* (Punk Hostage Press).

Growing up in Southern California provided much of the outlandish cartoon style that breathes throughout his work. Often playful with a bright bold color pallet his work falls mainly in the Pop Surreal or Kustom Culture genres. He collects Toys, Vinyl Records, Comics, Art Books and Guitars. He and his family moved to Texas. They love the open space and wildlife there and especially the southern hospitality. It's rough finding a good Pizza, but he's enjoying the pimento cheese sandwiches.

More Books on Punk Hostage Press

Danny Baker
  Fractured - 2012
A Razor
  Better Than a Gun in A Knife Fight - 2012
  *Drawn Blood: Collected   Works
  From D.B.P.LTD., 1985-1995* - 2012
  Beaten Up Beaten Down - 2012
  Small Catastrophes in A Big World - 2012
  Half- Century Status - 2013
  Days of Xmas Poems - 2014
  Puro Purismo - 2021
Iris Berry
  The Daughters of Bastards - 2012
  All That Shines Under the Hollywood Sign – 2019
  The Trouble with Palm Trees - 2021
C.V. Auchterlonie
  Impress - 2012
Yvonne De la Vega
  Tomorrow, Yvonne - Poetry & Prose for Suicidal Egoists - 2012
Carolyn Srygley- Moore
  Miracles of the Blog: A Series - 2012
Rich Ferguson
  8th & Agony -2012
Jack Grisham
  Untamed -2013
  Code Blue: A Love Story ~ 2014
  Pulse of the World. Arthur Chance, Punk Rock Detective - *2021*
Dennis Cruz
  Moth Wing Tea - 2013
  The Beast Is We - 2018
Frank Reardon
  Blood Music - 2013
Pleasant Gehman
  Showgirl Confidential – 2013
  *Rock 'N' Roll Witch – A Memoir of Sex Magick, Drugs
  and Rock 'N' Roll – 2022*
Michele McDannold
  Stealing The Midnight from A Handful of Days – 2014
Joel Landmine
  Yeah, Well... – 2014
  Things Change – 2021

More Books on Punk Hostage Press

www.ingramcontent.com/pod-product-compliance
Lightning Source LLC
Chambersburg PA
CBHW022347040426
42449CB00006B/765